Why "Theory for Everyone"?

Music Theory ("the study of how music works" - Wikipedia) can be a bit of a mystery to violin students. There is only one popular commercial string method book series in North America that even includes a dedicated theory workbook. Meanwhile, the violinists' piano-studying peers have sequential theory workbooks to go along with most popular lesson books. "Intervals" and "tetrachords" are terms and concepts that are introduced in most first year piano methods, and the Circle of Fifths is a handy and accessible tool for intermediate piano students and up. Many violin students will only achieve a rudimentary understanding of these concepts if they continue their studies to an advanced-intermediate level, if even then, because teachers don't have many published resources for teaching music theory to string players.

Music theory can and should be accessible to beginning violinists too! The payoff will come in better intonation (with deeper understanding of half and whole steps and other intervals), better music-reading (by relating key signatures to finger positions) and more expressive playing. Some students will enjoy their learning more if they get a glimpse "under the hood" into the WHYS of music-making. Some will experience an "Aha!" moment when they can relate their finger-positions to the piano keyboard's pattern of notes. And some will be empowered to write down their own compositions by obtaining access to the music-coding toolbox.

Created for all these students and more, "Theory for Everyone!" workbooks teach the sequential music theory concepts that naturally unfold when learning to play the violin. They blend with and overlay several popular beginners' teaching methods*, and improve on current published options with more practical focus and clarity of explanation, especially for younger students. The popular fill-in fingerboard charts and write-the-counting exercises are here, along with diagrams and exercises that I have not found effectively used in any available theory workbooks for violin, such as the relationship between the violin fingerboard and the piano keyboard, and the Circle of Fifths.

*such as All for Strings Books 1-2-3; Essential Elements Books 1-2-3 and similar

The: first tw first-pc signatt dotted eighth-sixteenth, triplets and syncopation, and 6/8 time signature. The Circle of Fifths at the end of Book Two is the takeaway tool that can provide much of the foundational understanding for advancing from here.

How to Use This Book

Book Two builds on the concepts presented in Book One, which thoroughly develops piano keyboard understanding as it relates to the violin fingerboard. Therefore some review of Book One may be necessary before completing the exercises in Book Two which require identification of notes on the keyboard. Book Two will match up with music theory concepts presented in most second-level method books and beyond. It is written at a little higher reading level than Book One, for older-elementary students and above. This 2nd Edition contains minor corrections and some added instructional materials.

Each short descriptive lesson ("Read It") in this book has an associated worksheet ("Write It") to apply the new knowledge to solve musical problems. Students should also play the visual examples in the lessons on their violin or keyboard when they see the "Do It" icon. The "Write It" worksheets are in their own section of the book so that students can fill out the worksheets with or without looking at the text for the answers. The teacher may allow "open-book" worksheet completion, or might use each worksheet as a test for whether the material was learned and understood. Underlined terms are defined in a glossary at the back of the book.

The worksheets can be photocopied and reworked as many times as necessary to achieve a 100% score. (Using sheet protectors with dry-erase pens saves paper!) An answer key is provided separately for fast corrections.   -- Jane Melin, NCTM

2nd Edition ©2019 G'DAE Music LLC
All Rights Reserved. Printed in U.S.A.
www.GDAEmusic.comwww.GDAEmusic.com

Theory for Everyone!

Practical Music Theory Lessons and Worksheets
for Beginning to Intermediate Violin Students

"A table, a chair, a bowl of fruit and a violin; what else does a man need to be happy?"
~ Albert Einstein, Theoretician

Table of Contents

Book One Review

If you are new to the <u>Theory for Everyone</u> series, here are some of the visual and musical concepts presented in Book One that you will need to understand before going on to Book Two.

The Treble Clef Staff

with Line/Space note name assignments

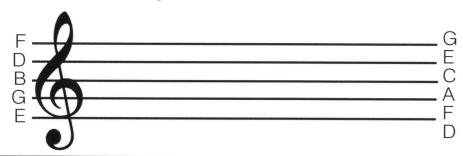

The Violin Fingerboard

String labels across the top;
finger numbers down the side

The "home notes" are circles on the fingerboard diagram. Extended notes (Low 2, High 3 etc.) are octagons. When enharmonic notes are introduced, the finger locations where "notes with two names" are played will have a diagonal line through them:

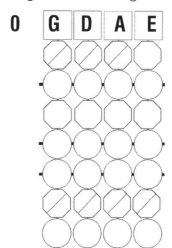

Violin Notes on the Piano Keyboard

from open G string to 4th finger on E string

Same notes as on fingerboard diagram above (high 2nd fingers). Open string notes are circled and piano Middle C is starred.

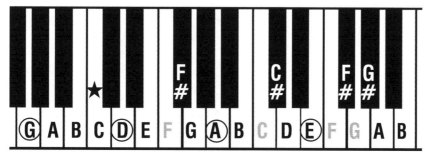

1. Tetrachords, Scales and Modes

Every culture's music follows its own rules and patterns. When it does, it sounds "right" to the listeners' ears, because that's the music they've heard since infancy. If we've been immersed in music from the Western European tradition, the pattern we follow to build *Do-Re-Mi* major scales is just one of many possible patterns, but it is the one we are most used to hearing. Here's how the pattern works:

A <u>major tetrachord</u> is a series of four notes with a pattern between the notes of WHOLE STEP, WHOLE STEP, HALF STEP or **W-W-H** . (The four notes of a tetrachord must always be neighboring letters of the musical alphabet; i.e. D E F♯ G, not D E G♭ G.) The <u>major scale</u> is made of TWO TETRACHORDS joined together by a WHOLE STEP. Here is the pattern for a C major scale, the white notes on a piano keyboard:

C   D   E   F | G   A   B   C

1st tetrachord   2nd tetrachord   Shorthand pattern: **W W H W W W H**

And here is the D major scale pattern, the scale you would play starting on the open D string:

D   E   F♯ G | A   B   C♯ D

This pattern works regardless of which note is the first one in the scale. It is how we build the major scale from any <u>key note</u> (the root, first, or primary note of the scale).

Relating this pattern to violin fingering:
If you play a one-octave (eight-note) major scale that starts on any of the lower three open strings (G, D or A), your fingers will follow the same pattern on each string pair: **0-1-23-0-1-23**. Dashes represent a whole-step space between two fingers or notes. If you break the scale in half, you can see that each half follows the same pattern: **0-1-23**. There are whole steps (W) following the 1st and 2nd notes and a half step (H) between the 3rd and 4th -- this is the major tetrachord again. A whole step joins the two tetrachords, between 3rd finger and the next open string. If you had eight fingers and started the scale on finger #1, the pattern of close-and-far fingers would be **1-2-34-5-6-78**.

Remember the question, "why are there no sharps between B-C and E-F" from Book 1? To play a C-major scale on the keyboard, you start on C and play all the white keys up to the next C. Looking at the pattern of whole- and half-steps, you'll see that the white keys are joined together in the double-tetrachord sequence described above. Because the tetrachord sequence isn't perfectly regular (as in all-whole-steps or all-half-steps), neither is the white/black key pattern on the keyboard.

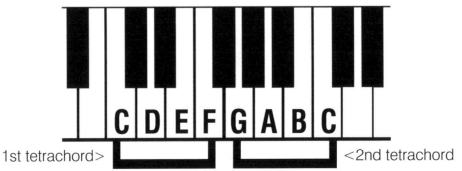

1st tetrachord>   <2nd tetrachord

Modes: Major, Minor and More

Most Western classical and pop music is written in either the <u>major</u> or <u>minor</u> mode. Your ears are tuned for major ("happy") and minor ("sad") modes by long exposure. A <u>mode</u> refers to a type of scale from which tunes are constructed. Music in unfamiliar modes may sound like it is missing sharps or flats, or ends on the wrong note. Playing folk music from Celtic or Eastern European cultures, or listening to medieval chants or motets are ways to experience music in these modes.

The Minor Mode on the Keyboard

Every mode has a different pattern of half- and whole-steps in an 8-note scale. The <u>natural minor mode</u> follows this pattern: **1-23-4-56-7-8** or **(Root note)-Whole-Half-Whole-Whole-Half-Whole-Whole.** (Shorthand: **W H W W H W W**). On a piano, notes follow this pattern if you start on **A** and play all the white keys to the next **A**. This probably sounds "sad": it is the A Minor scale. On the keyboard below, there are half-steps between **B-C** and **E-F**; these are the 2nd-3rd and 5th-6th notes of the scale.

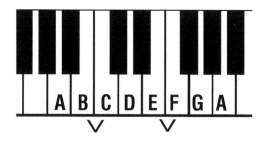

Using the same note-pattern and starting on the note B, the B natural minor scale has a C# and an F#: the same sharps as the key of D major. We'll explore related major and minor keys in #14.

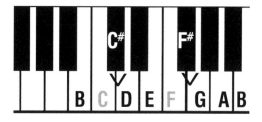

Every mode has a different Greek name. The <u>major mode</u> is also known as the *Ionian.* It follows the pattern of the white keys starting on **C**. The <u>minor mode</u> is called the *Aeolian* and the pattern starts on **A** (as above). The *Dorian* mode is a scale of the white keys starting on **D**. There are four more named modes: *Mixolydian, Phrygian, Lydian* and *Locrian.* You can play the pattern for each mode by starting on a different white key than the ones already listed. Explore more about modes here: http://en.wikipedia.org/wiki/Mode_(music)

Do Write it #1.

2. Low 2's

To play all the possible notes in first position, each finger will eventually learn to play two different notes on each string. Notes that are not part of the original **0-1-23-4** pattern will be marked on the fingerboard charts with an octagon ◯ instead of a circle. Many method books start with a new note for the second finger. These notes are played by placing the second finger "low," just in front of the first finger, leaving a space before the third finger. This finger pattern can be written **0-12-3-4** where dashes represent whole steps.

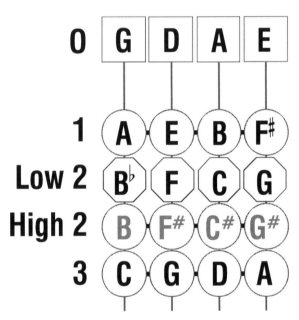

You will use this Low 2 finger position when you want to play the following notes:

(On D:) F♮ (F natural) instead of F♯

(On A:) C♮ instead of C♯

(On E:) G♮ instead of G♯

(On G:) B♭ instead of B♮ (this will be covered in the upcoming section on Flats, #10)

How do you know when you need to play Low 2 notes? The answer always lies in the key signature. Now you'll need to look for what is missing, as well as what is there. When F♯, C♯ and G♯ are <u>not</u> in the key signature, you'll use Low 2 on the D string, A string and E string, in that order. When there's a flat sign ♭ on the staff line for B, a Low 2 is needed on the G string (more on that in #13).

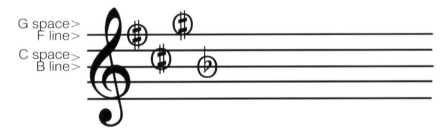

The circles on the staff represent where to look for the sharps and a flat that change the 2nd finger's placement.

No G♯: Low 2 on E

No C♯: Low 2 on A and E

No F♯: Low 2 on D, A and E

B♭: Low 2 on <u>all the strings</u>

3. The Key of G

Before learning how to place the 2nd finger in the "low" position, you would only have been able to play one-octave (8-note) scales that start on an open string. You wouldn't have known enough notes to play complete scales in other keys. After learning Low 2, you can play a 2-octave scale that starts on the open G string and goes up to Low 2 on the E string. This scale also requires a Low 2 on the A string, but High 2's on the G and D strings.

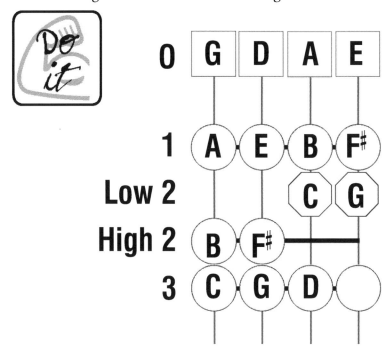

Only one note in this scale has a sharp sign next to it: the note F. In other words, F♯ is the only sharp in this scale. Here is how to write the <u>key signature</u> for music that uses notes from the G-major scale:

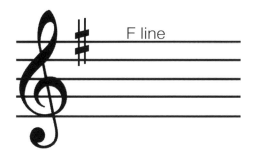

From now on when you start a new piece of music, play close attention to the key signature. It will tell you whether to use High or Low 2's, and on which strings. Later it will also tell you when to use Low 1's, Low 4's and High 3's, so get used to reading and decoding key signatures!

Do **Write it** #3.

Theory for Everyone • Violin Book 2

4. Arpeggios Beyond 1 Octave

In Book One #12, the Arpeggio was introduced as a fundamental musical pattern that all composers use. This "broken chord" pattern allows single-note instruments to simulate the harmonic qualities of instruments that can play complete chords, like pianos and guitars. The word "arpeggio" means "to play like a harp."

The basic arpeggio that goes with each key starts on the <u>first</u> note of the scale, then goes to the <u>third</u> note, then the <u>fifth</u> note, then up to the top note of the scale -- which is a repetition of the first note, one octave higher. (This pattern is a broken form of the tonic triad chord.) To play arpeggios of more than one octave, continue to stack the notes 1, 3, 5 as high as you can play -- then go back down the same notes, like descending a ladder, to the starting note.

After learning the 2-octave G Major scale, you can play its 2-octave arpeggio. The notes of the G Major scale are **G̲ A B̲ C D̲ E F♯ G.**

Notes 1, 3 and 5 are: **G̲, B̲, D̲**

The top G of the first octave is the bottom note (Note 1) of the next octave. The full 2-octave arpeggio is played 1-3-5//1-3-5//1//5-3-1//5-3-1:

Here are the notes of the G major arpeggio on the fingerboard, and on a keyboard:

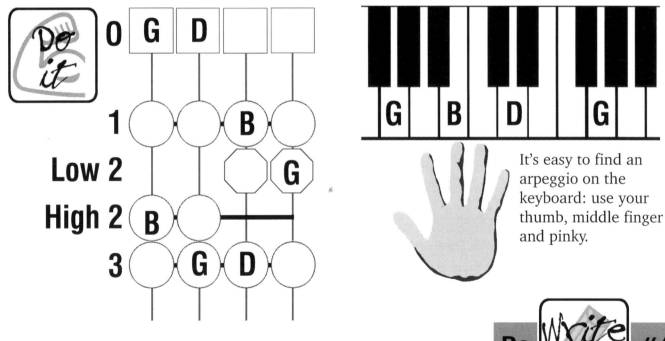

It's easy to find an arpeggio on the keyboard: use your thumb, middle finger and pinky.

Do **Write it** #4.

5. The Key of C

The next key signature to decode has no sharps OR flats. This is the Key of C, a major scale you can play from 3rd finger on the G string to Low 2 on the A string. This is the first key that piano students learn, because it uses only white-key-notes. It takes awhile for violin students to get to this point, because the Key of C requires using Low 2 on three strings: D, A and E. (But still High 2 on the G string.)

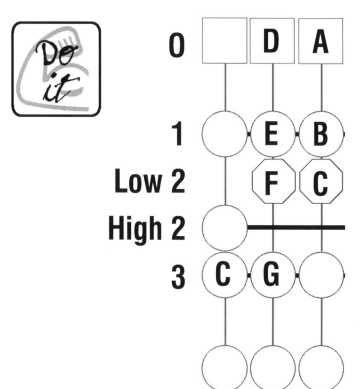

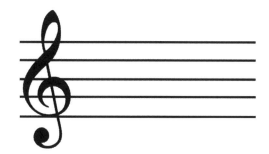

Here is the key signature for C: NO SHARPS or flats!

Key of C on the keyboard:

Do Write it #5.

6. Syncopation

So far when we've played eighth notes, they've come in pairs joined together by a beam: ♩♩. (Remember that single eighth notes have a flag attached to the stem: ♪) When counting pairs of eighth notes that start on the beat, the first one is called by the number of the beat and the second one is called "and." We could also use the symbol &.

When two eighth notes are separated by a quarter note, the uneven-sounding rhythm is called <u>syncopation</u>. Here is a syncopated rhythm: ♪ ♩ ♪. To count this, remember that there are two eighth notes inside each quarter note. If this pattern starts on beat 1, count ♪ ♩ ♪ . "And 2" are the two eighth notes inside the quarter note.   1   and 2 and

Here is a longer syncopated pattern with counting in 4/4 time. A tune that fits this rhythm is called "Lil' Liza Jane."

7. 6/8 Time Signature

Here's another situation where you'll need to count individual eighth notes. Remember that time signatures show the number of beats in the measure on the <u>top</u> and the kind of note that gets the beat on the <u>bottom</u>. So in 3/4 time, there are 3 beats per measure and quarter notes (¼) get the counted beats.

How about §? There are __6__ beats per measure (top number) and __8th__ notes are counted. The type of note counted is the number from the bottom of the time signature turned into a fraction with a 1 on top: 1/8 (eighth).

When eighth notes ♪ are counted, one beat per eighth note, remember to count:

⅞ = 1 beat rest   ♩ or 𝄽 = 2 beats   ♩. or 𝄽. = 3 beats   𝅗𝅥 or ▬ = 4 beats   𝅗𝅥. = 6 beats

Dividing one eighth-note into two makes two sixteenth notes: ♬. In 6/8 time, this pair of notes is counted like eighth notes are when quarter notes get the beat: "1-and-2-and" etc.

8. High 3's and All the Sharps

By learning to place the third finger a half-step higher than its "home" position, you can play several new notes. Crossing from the G to the E string, these notes are: C♯, G♯, D♯ and A♯.

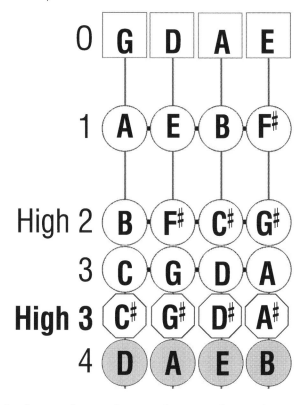

Now you can play in the keys of D and A on the G and D strings. Why? Because these keys call for C♯ and G♯. Here are the key signatures, with the sharps that change your 3rd fingers circled:

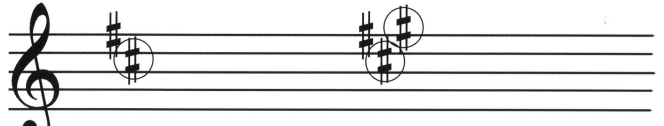

Key of D:
High 3rd finger **C♯** on G string

Key of A:
High 3rd fingers **C♯** on G string and **G♯** on D string

Here are all 5 sharps from the fingerboard chart above, located on the keyboard's black notes.

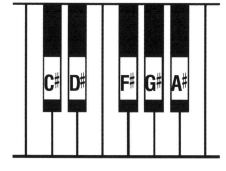

Do  #8.

9. Key of E

The key signature that warns of "High 3's Ahead" has four sharps. This is the signature for the key of E. If you play a major scale starting on 1st finger on the D-string (E) and going up to the open E string, you will play both G♯ and D♯ (High 3's on the D and A strings). You'll also need High 3 on the G string (C♯) in this key.

Here is how the sharps F-C-G-D are positioned on the staff:

And, the notes of the E major scale on the fingerboard:

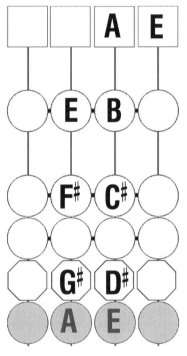

This workbook only takes you as far as the 4-sharp key signature. There are 3 more possible sharps to add—A, E and B—before we've sharped all 7 natural notes. It's sometimes helpful to memorize a catchy phrase to remember the order of the sharps in the key signature, from left to right. Here is one phrase that many music students have used: **F**at **C**ats **G**o **D**own **A**lleys **E**ating **B**ugs.

Do  #9.

Theory for Everyone • Violin Book 2

10. Flats and Enharmonics

<u>Flats</u> are notes which are a half-step <u>below</u> a natural note. The symbol for "Flat" is ♭ . Remember that every note which is a sharp when looking at it from one direction — up the piano keyboard (or violin fingerboard) from a natural note — is a flat when looking at it from the other direction — down. In other words, another name for G♯ (a half-step up from G natural) is A♭ (a half-step down from A natural). G♯ and A♭ are <u>enharmonic notes</u>—notes that are written differently but sound the same. (Similar to "homophones," words that sound the same but have different spellings and meanings, like "dear" and "deer.")

The best way to illustrate enharmonic notes is with the piano keyboard. You can see that there's only one black note (at most) between any two white notes, so it has to serve as a *flat* for one and a *sharp* for the other.

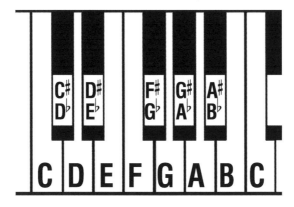

You're about to learn a couple new finger positions for your 4th and 1st fingers so you'll be able to play music written in key signatures with flats.

Do Write it #10.

11. Low 4's

When the 4th finger is brought in close to the 3rd finger — a half-step away — it is called "Low 4." Usually the notes played with Low 4 are flats. The names of these notes are easy to remember: they are the next-higher open string name plus "flat". Low 4 on the E string is B♭. (So if there were one higher string on a violin, it would be a B string!)

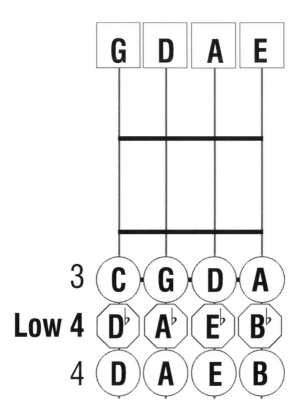

Notice that these notes are in exactly the same place on the fingerboard as the High 3's. (Remember "enharmonic notes"?) Why then do you need to learn a new finger position to cover these notes?

The answer is: When you're playing in a key with flats that requires Low 4, you will also almost always be using a Low 1st finger (see next section) and a Low 2 a whole step from your first finger. Your 3 will be needed in its original position. Rather than requiring the third finger to play two different notes, "regular" 3 and "high" 3, which stretches far away from your Low 2, you'll call on your fourth finger to cover this spot instead.

When playing in keys with several sharps (the keys of A, E etc.), the 1 and 2 are in their original positions and the 3 goes to its High position; using Low 4 instead would leave the 3rd finger without a job.

Do #11.

12. Low 1's

The secondary position for your 1st finger is called "Low 1." You'll place your 1st finger approximately halfway between its original position and the nut (the raised edge where the string emerges from the peg box). This lowers your regular 1st-finger notes by a half-step so you can play the following notes, crossing from the G to the E string: A♭, E♭, B♭, F (F natural).

Remember that the regular 1st-finger note on the E string is F♯, so going down a half-step takes you to F♮. (See #1 to review the reason why!)

Each of these Low 1 notes has an enharmonic twin. Can you fill in the blanks here and in the fingerboard chart?

A♭ = _____♯   E♭ = _____♯   B♭ = _____♯   F = _____♯ ???

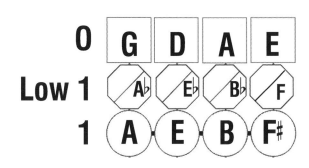

(Add enharmonic names in the upper half of the Low 1 boxes)

Answers: G♯, D♯, A♯, E♯

Do Write it #12.

Theory for Everyone • Violin Book 2

13. Keys of F, B♭, E♭

Here are the key signatures that require the use of Low 4's and Low 1's. Low 2's are also marked on the fingerboard charts*.

Key of F = 1 flat: **B♭**; Low 1 on A and E strings; Low 4 on E string; Low 2 on G string

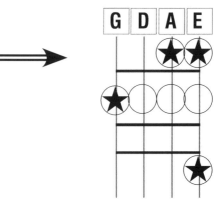

Key of B♭ = 2 flats: **B♭** and **E♭**; add Low 1 on D; Low 4 on A

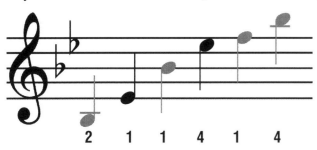

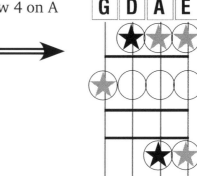

Key of E♭ = 3 flats: **B♭**, **E♭** and **A♭**; add Low 1 on G; Low 4 on D; *Low 3 on E*

Special case, "half position"

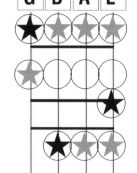

*Note that all of these keys require Low 2's, because High 2's need sharps and a B-natural (that is, absence of B♭) in the key signature.

Just as when learning the order in which sharps are written into the key signature, there's a phrase to help you remember the order of flats: **B**-**E**-**A**-**D**-**G**eese-**C**an-**F**ly.

Key signatures of more than three flats are uncommon in beginning violin method books, but you'll be prepared when you see them for the first time. Wind instrument students often learn flats before sharps, so if you are playing in a mixed ensemble or orchestra, you may have to play music in key signatures with flats to accommodate the wind players.

Theory for Everyone • Violin Book 2

14. Minor Scales: Natural, Melodic, Harmonic

Review *Read It #1* for a quick overview of the <u>minor mode</u>. Remember that the <u>natural minor mode</u> follows this scale pattern: **1-23-4-56-7-8** [Root-**W H W W H W W**]. On a piano, if you start on A and play all the white keys to the next A, the notes follow this pattern and it *sounds like* a minor scale. This scale is A minor; the notes you played are the notes of the C major scale, so A is called the <u>relative minor</u> of C major. **The relative minor of any key is two notes below (or six notes above) the original key note,** *in the scale of the original key.*

There are two more note-sequence patterns that are considered "minor." The <u>melodic minor</u> includes a few notes from the major key on the way up the scale, and takes the natural minor pattern on the way back down. In fact, the place where the scale switches from the natural-minor notes to the major key notes is in the <u>second tetrachord</u> going up.

Ascending: **1-23-4-5-6-78**   Descending: **8-7-65-4-32-1**

minor tetrachord + major tetrachord   two minor tetrachords

Here is what the **A** <u>melodic minor</u> scale looks like on the piano keyboard. **A** major has three sharps: F#, C# and G#. The melodic minor uses F# and G# on the way up, then goes back to "no sharps" (C major's key signature) on the way down.

The <u>harmonic minor</u> scale pattern is the same as the natural minor, except the seventh note of the scale is raised a half-step. This puts a step-and-a-half between the 6th and 7th notes of the scale: **1-23-4-56—78**. The sound of this scale might remind you of Middle Eastern music or the "snake charmer" theme. The harmonic minor uses the same notes going both up and down. Here is what an **A** <u>harmonic minor scale</u> looks like on the piano keyboard.

Quick Reference for Major and Minor Scale Note-Spacing Patterns:

Major	**1-2-34-5-6-78**	or (Root) **W W H W W W H**
Natural minor	**1-23-4-56-7-8**	or (Root) **W H W W H W W**
Melodic minor	Up: **1-23-4-5-6-78**	Down: **8-7-65-4-32-1**
	Up: (Root) **W H W W W W H**	Down: (Top) **W W H W W H W**
Harmonic minor	**1-23-4-56—78**	or (Root) **W H W W H W+H H**

In all minor scales, the spacing of the first 5 notes (first tetrachord plus a whole step) is the same. It is in the second tetrachord where the spacing changes.

Do  #14.

15. Important Intervals

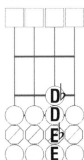

An <u>interval</u> is the <u>distance between two notes</u> expressed as a number. The half step and the whole step are both intervals. Another name for each of them is a <u>minor second</u> (half step) and a <u>major second</u> (whole step). The term "second" is used for both of these intervals because they describe two notes that are separated by one <u>degree</u> from each other: in the music alphabet, from one letter to the next; on the staff, from a space-note to a line-note or a line-note to a space-note. When describing intervals, the terms <u>minor</u> and <u>major,</u> or sometimes <u>diminished</u> and <u>augmented,</u> are used to describe the closeness of two notes that share the same interval degree number. For example, the interval D to E is a second (2nd), but there can be differences of degree if one of the notes is flatted: D to E is a <u>major second</u> (whole step), D to E♭ is a <u>minor second</u> (half step), D♭ to E is an <u>augmented</u> second (step-and-a-half).

The most familiar intervals on the violin are the <u>fifth</u> (or perfect fifth) and the <u>octave</u>. The violin is tuned in <u>fifths</u>—each string is five notes away from the string on either side. The distance from one note to the next note that has the same name is an <u>octave</u>. Octaves can be found on the violin from an open string to the 3rd finger on the next higher string, such as from open D to 3rd-finger D on the A string.

When you start to learn how to play double-stops, you will learn other intervals such as major and minor thirds, major and minor sixths, fourths, and sevenths. Here are some illustrations of the different intervals on the keyboard for easier visualization.

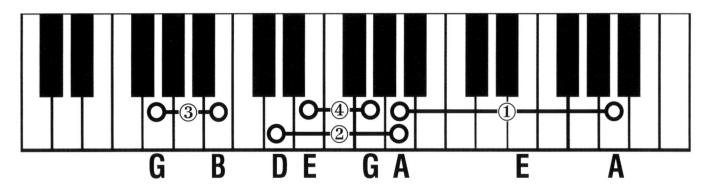

① A to A: Octave, 12 half-steps

② D to A: Perfect fifth, 7 half-steps

③ G to B: Major third, 4 half-steps. When playing a G <u>major</u> scale, B is the <u>third</u> note (<u>major</u> <u>third</u>)

④ E to G: Minor third, 3 half-steps. The major third would be from E to G#, 4 half-steps. When playing an E <u>minor</u> scale, G is the <u>third</u> note (<u>minor</u> <u>third</u>). G# is the third note of an <u>E major</u> scale.

Do **#15.**

Theory for Everyone • Violin Book 2

16. Sixteenth Notes

We've divided note lengths into half several times already: from whole notes to half notes, quarter notes and eighth notes. The next division creates sixteenth notes, 1/16. Sixteenth notes are drawn by adding another flag to a single eighth note ♪, or another bar to a pair or more of eighth notes: ♬ or ♬♬ .

Here's the pizza once again, divided into 16 slices. How many 16ths in an eighth (1/8)?

_____

In a fourth (1/4)? _____

In a half (1/2)? _____

One quarter-note is worth four sixteenth-notes.

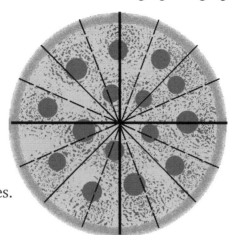

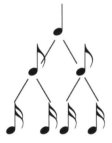

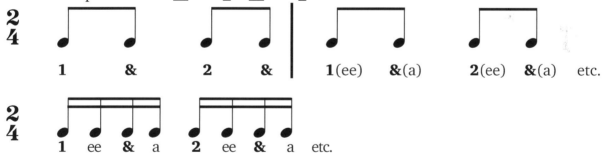

To count sixteenth notes, we insert two more syllables into the "1-and-2-and" pattern used to count eighth-notes and expand it to "1-ee-and-a-2-ee-and-a".

Sixteenth notes are most commonly written in groups of four or two. If a group of two sixteenth notes comes before or after an eighth note, the notes are usually joined together with a straight line called a <u>beam</u> to link one whole beat, which is counted this way:

Clap Quarter, Eighth and Sixteenth note subdivisions to a metronome beat of 60 BPM to the quarter note. Say the rhythm syllables out loud to the beat.

Theory for Everyone • Violin Book 2

17. Dotted Eighth + Sixteenth Notes

Having fractional notes as small as a quarter of a beat (i.e. sixteenth notes) allows for many rhythmic combinations of longer and shorter notes together. One of the most common is the dotted-eighth + sixteenth pair. This is a faster version of the long-short pattern of dotted-quarter + eighth-note (see Book One # 19). Once again, the dot next to an eighth note adds half the value of the eighth note; that is, a sixteenth note. Here are the steps to get to this rhythmic pattern:

It is important to recognize that the first note of this pair, the dotted eighth note, is three 16th-notes long, and the last note is just one 16th note. When playing this note pair, make sure you sustain the first note three times longer than the second. It is easy to get "lazy" and play the first note just two times longer than the second; the effect is of playing grouped <u>triplets</u>, not sixteenth notes.

Do **Write it** #17.

18. Triplets*

(*eighth note triplets)

Feeling a musical pulse subdivided into groups of threes often happens when playing music in 6/8 time. This is because the "big beats" of 6/8 are dotted quarter notes, which have 3 eighth notes inside. The 6/8 folk song "Greensleeves" can be counted like this, with "big beats" on 1 and 4:

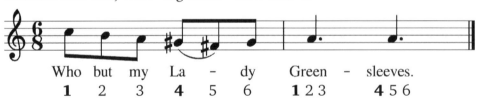

To get the same feel in 4/4, we need to divide quarter notes into three equal parts. These are called <u>triplets</u>. A single triplet is shorter than an eighth note, but longer than a 16th note. *There are 12 of them in a whole note!* Here is the last measure of "Greensleeves" written with triplets, and a suggested way to count them:

Since triplets look just like eighth notes, the main way to tell the difference is to look for a number "3" next to the note beams. (Do you see it?) A careful music transcriber will always write this **3** to help the reader spot the triplets. If the "3" is missing, the only other way to tell is <u>math</u>. If the example above were composed of eighth notes instead of triplets, there would be 5 beats in the 4/4 measure!

Do **Write it** #18.

Theory for Everyone • Violin Book 2

19. Note-Name Review

Here is a completed fingerboard chart showing all the notes you've learned to play in first position. With these notes, you can now play music with any number of sharps or flats, as long as the highest note is B on the E string. For higher notes, you will need to learn to play above first position, which is beyond the scope of this workbook. However, the knowledge you've gained about the arrangement of notes and the distances between them will help you immensely as you learn how to find notes with a new starting first-finger position.

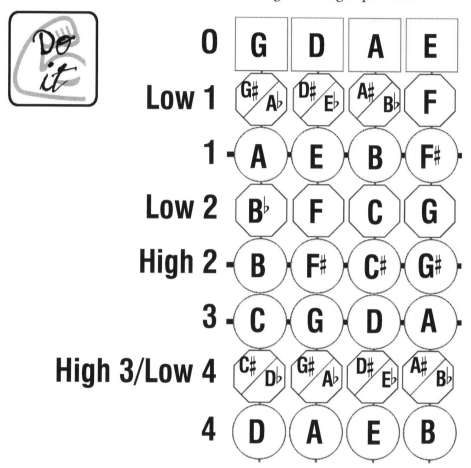

What are the enharmonic names of the sharped High 2 notes? (sometimes played with Low 3, in keys with three or more flats)

Low 2 on the G string and "regular" 1 on the E string also have enharmonic names, but students will rarely play in keys that require reading these notes as something other than B-flat and F-sharp.

Do Write it #19.

20. The Circle of Fifths: Order of Sharps & Flats

The order of sharps and the order of flats can be diagrammed by drawing a circle with all the possible note-names arranged around it like a clock. This tool is called the "Circle of Fifths" and is very helpful for more advanced music theory understanding, including chord progressions and recognizing the three main chords that go with every key. (Beginning guitar players learn these 3-chord groups from the very start.)

The Circle of Fifths is arranged with C-natural at the top. C is the key of no sharps and no flats, so it is "neutral" on the circle and gets to sit at the 12:00 position. Going around the circle clockwise are the keys that add sharps; going around counterclockwise are the keys that add flats. At the bottom are where the sharps and flats overlap, and there are two enharmonic keys noted.

To use the memorable phrases you've already learned to master the Circle of Fifths, start one position to the left of C (11:00) and put F there. Now you can write the first letters of the phrase "**F**at **C**ats **G**o **D**own **A**lleys **E**ating **B**ugs" going clockwise — to the right. G is the key with one sharp; D is the key with 2; A is the key with 3 and so on. *Do you see a pattern that matches the strings on the violin?*

Going around the other way (counterclockwise), start to the left of F (at the 10:00 position) and write the first letters of "**B-E-A-D-G**eese-**C**an-**F**ly", together with a flat sign next to each letter. You'll see that the last two letters overlap with the first set; C♭ is the same as B♮, and F♭ is also E♮. (These are the same letter pairs that have "no black key" between!) From the left side of C going counterclockwise, the key signatures add flats, from F (one flat) to B♭ (two flats), to E♭ (three flats) and so on.

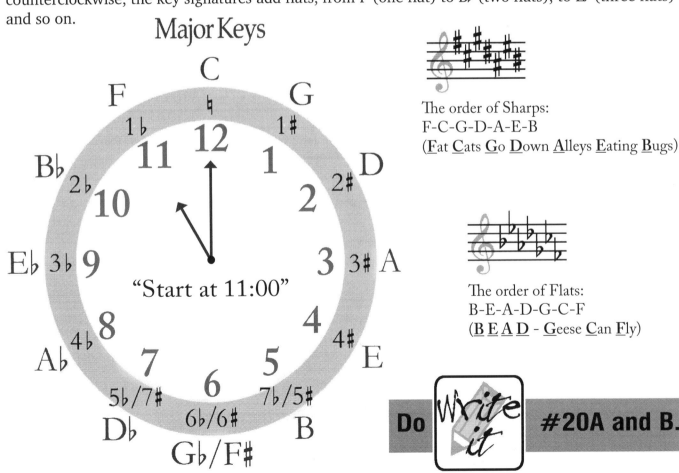

Major Keys

The order of Sharps:
F-C-G-D-A-E-B
(**F**at **C**ats **G**o **D**own **A**lleys **E**ating **B**ugs)

The order of Flats:
B-E-A-D-G-C-F
(**B E A D** - **G**eese **C**an **Fl**y)

Do [Write it] #20A and B.

21. Relative Minors on the Circle of Fifths

The Circle of Fifths also helps identify the relative minor keys for each major key. The minor key with no sharps or flats is A-minor, so it also goes in the 12:00 position along with C-major. When identified by a single letter, major keys are written with capital letters (C = C major) and minor keys are written lower-case (a = A minor). The phrases you've memorized can be used again to place the relative minors around the circle to match up with their majors. If you remember that "a" is at 12:00 and its position in the order of "Fat Cats Go Down Alleys Eating Bugs" OR "B-E-A-D-Geese-Can-Fly", you can fill in the missing letters. Just remember that "Fat Cats" runs clockwise and BEAD runs counterclockwise, so that you put them in the right order.

In the upper half of the circle are the minor keys that start on natural notes. The lower half gets more complicated, because some of these are keys with flats and some are with sharps, and you'll end up in enharmonic keys eventually. (Chances are you won't be playing many pieces in the key of G♯-minor for some time, but when you do, you'll recognize it sounds the same as A♭-minor.) Check your work: how many sharps/flats in the key of D minor? E minor?

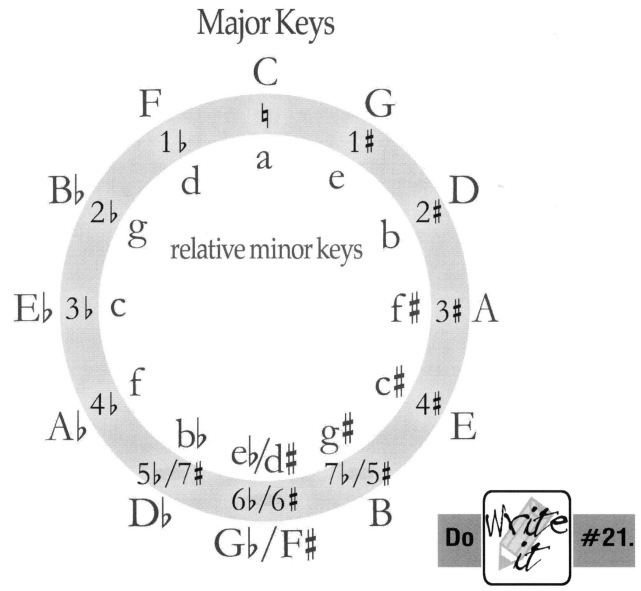

22. The Circle of Fifths and I-IV-V Chords

Chords are groups of notes played at the same time to create harmonies. Double-stops familiar to violinists are a simple type of chord; so are arpeggios, which are also called <u>broken chords</u>. Pianists, who can play more than two notes at a time, become familiar with many types of chords. The most basic chords are the major and minor <u>triads</u>: a set of three notes which are the first, third and fifth note of a major or minor scale.

The Circle of Fifths is a helpful tool for composers and improvisers such as jazz musicians, because it shows which chords are most closely related to any key. Lots of popular music contains only three different chords for an entire song; beginning guitar players who learn three basic chords can accompany a lot of music, as long as it's in the key they're playing!

Triad chords I, IV and V for the key of G with their names labeled above

These chords are named by the first, fourth and fifth notes of the key's major scale, and are designated by the Roman numerals I, IV and V. The first or bottom note in each 3-note chord or <u>triad</u> is note number I, IV or V of the scale. The next two notes are 3 and 5 notes up from the bottom note of the chord, treating the bottom note as the beginning of a new scale in its own key.

To illustrate, let's take three basic triad chords, the ones for the key of G, which has one sharp. The fourth note (IV) of a G major scale is C, and the fifth note (V) is D. And if you go five notes down from G, that note is also a C. So it's no surprise that on the Circle of Fifths, C is just to the left of G and D is just to the right. Why are these particular chords perfect for the key of G? The notes in a C-chord are C, E and G. The notes for a D-chord are D, F# and A. The G-chord notes are G, B and D. That covers all the notes in a G-major scale, with a little bit of overlap. So no matter what note of the melody is sung or played, as long as the melody note is one of the notes in a G-major scale, there is a chord that has that note in it.

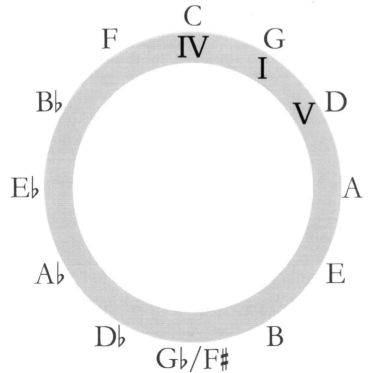

Using the Circle of Fifths, can you identify the three main chords (I, IV, V) for a tune in the key of D? The key of C? The key of E?

E: E,A,B
C: C,F,G
D: D,G,A

To hear violins imitating the sound of guitars playing chords in the key of G, find a recording of the string quintet called "Night Music of the Streets of Madrid" by Luigi Boccherini. In the second movement, the violins are strumming the chords G, C and D.

Do #22.

The Circle of Fifths - Complete

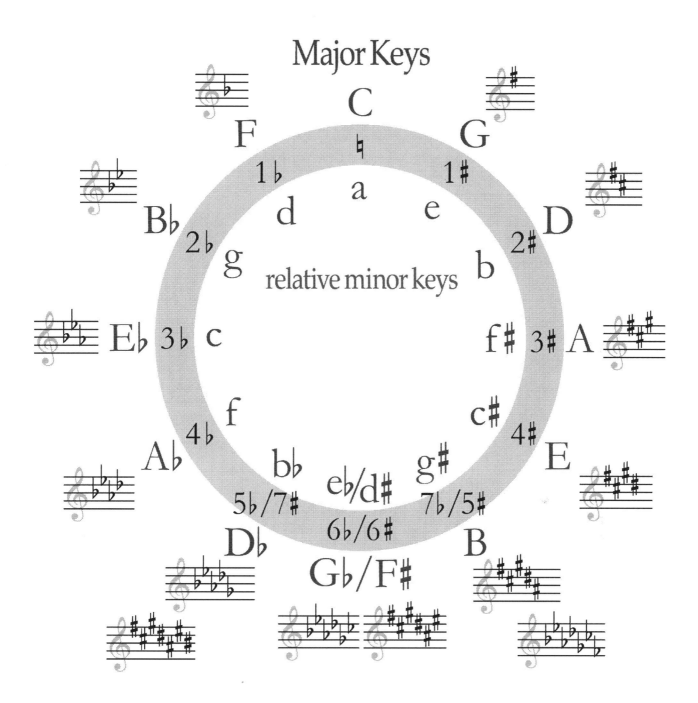

The order of Sharps:
F-C-G-D-A-E-B (**F**at **C**ats **G**o **D**own **A**lleys **E**ating **B**ugs)

The order of Flats:
B-E-A-D-G-C-F (**B** **E** **A** **D** - **G**eese **C**an **F**ly)

Theory for Everyone • Violin Book 2

1. Tetrachords and Scales

Write it

Follow the major tetrachord pattern (**1-2-34-5-6-78**) where dashes represent whole steps between notes, and use the keyboard example in the Book One Review. Mark X's on the notes for a one-octave <u>D major scale</u> on this keyboard:

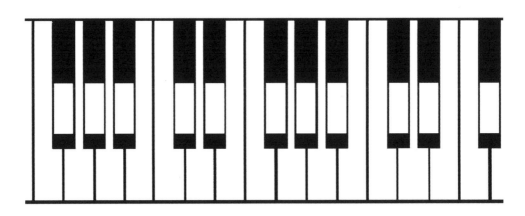

Now, try a one-octave <u>F major scale</u>:

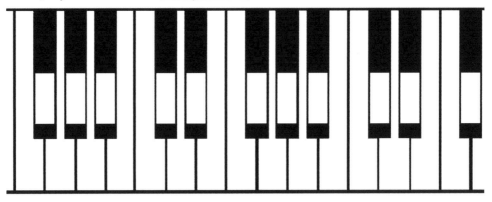

Using what you learned on page 3, mark X's on the notes for a one octave <u>D natural minor scale</u>.

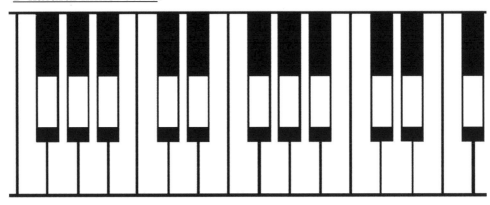

2. Low 2's

A. Write note names inside the circles for Low 2's and High 2's, open strings, 1's and 3's. Include sharp and flat signs where needed.

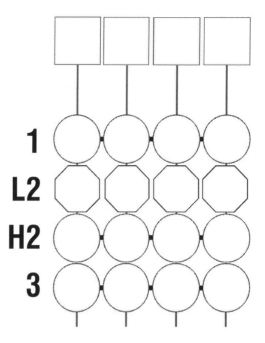

B. 1) Label each note with its alphabet letter name above the staff. 2) Circle the line or space on the staff where a sharp or flat would go that would change the position of the second finger in each example. 3) Write the sharp sign or flat sign in your circle. 4) Circle where the flat or sharp puts the 2nd finger: High or Low?

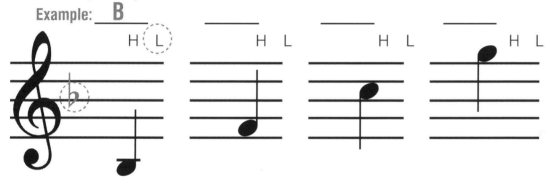

C. Under each note, write **H** if it's played with high 2 or **L** if it's low 2, based on each key signature.

Theory for Everyone • Violin Book 2 Worksheets

3. The Key of G

A. Write the names of the notes in a two-octave G major scale from open G to G on the E-string. Only write note-names on the notes that are in the scale; remember, some 2's are high and some are low. Use sharp signs (#) when needed.

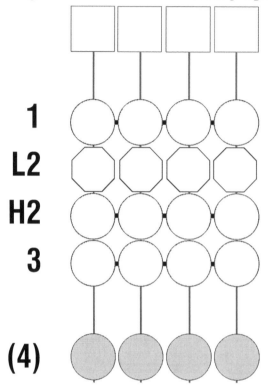

B. Write the one sharp for the Key of G on the staff.

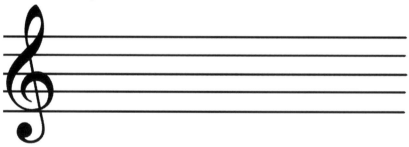

C. Write the names of the notes in the G major scale from the lowest G on this keyboard through two octaves to the highest G. Include the correct sharp. (Same notes as in A, above.)

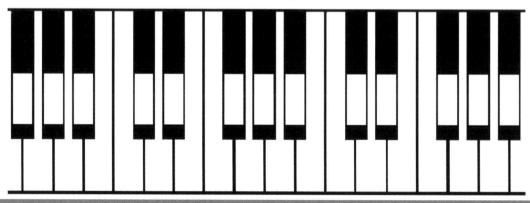

Theory for Everyone • Violin Book 2 Worksheets

4. Arpeggios Beyond 1 Octave

A. Write the names of the notes of an A major scale: one octave only, include sharps. Then circle notes 1, 3 and 5.

_____

B. Using the notes circled above, write the names of the arpeggio notes, beginning and ending on A and going up for **2** octaves and then down (include sharps):

_____

C.   Write the key signature for A major on the staff, then write the A major 2-octave arpeggio, up and down, with quarter notes. Place the stems on the correct side and direction for each note. Then, play the arpeggio.

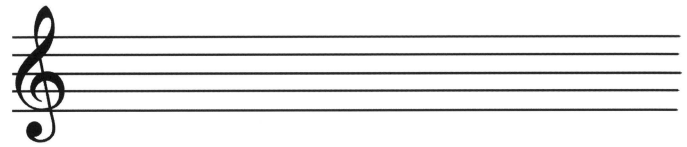

D. TEACHER'S CHOICE: Assign written arpeggios of 1 or 2 octaves in any other keys that have been studied. Student should play each arpeggio to check for errors.

Key_____

Key_____

Key_____

5. The Key of C

A. Write the names of the notes in a C major scale through one octave on the keyboard. Start on a C.

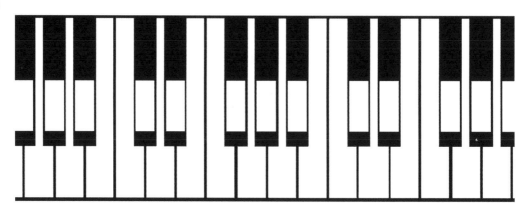

B. Write the names of the notes in a C major scale from C on the G string to C on the A string. Only write the names of the notes that are in the scale. Remember which 2's are low.

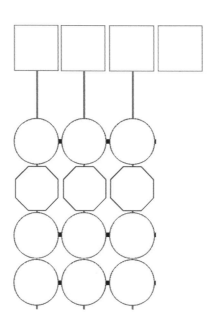

Theory for Everyone • Violin Book 2 Worksheets

6. Syncopation

Write the counting under this syncopated musical phrase and insert the bar lines.
Can you identify this familiar piece of music by its rhythm?

7. 6/8 Time

A. How many beats do each of these notes and rests get in $\frac{6}{8}$ time?

B. Write the counting under this portion of a familiar $\frac{6}{8}$ song's rhythm, insert the bar lines and try to identify it. (It's the second half of the tune.)

Theory for Everyone • Violin Book 2 Worksheets

8. High 3's and All the Sharps

A. Write note names inside the circles and octagons for normal 3's and High 3's, open strings, 4th fingers (in the gray circles), 1's and High 2's. Include sharp and flat signs where needed.

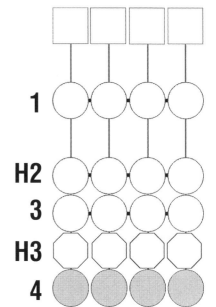

B. See example in *Write It #2*.
1) Label each note with its alphabet-letter name above the staff.
2) Circle the line or space on the staff where a sharp would go that would change the position of the third finger in each example.
3) Write the sharp sign in your circle.

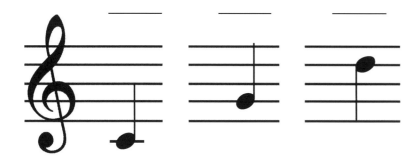

C. Under each note, write **H** if it's played with high 3 or **L** if it's low 3 (i.e. in its original place), based on each key signature.

D. Write sharp names on all black keys. Remember that sharps are to the right of naturals.

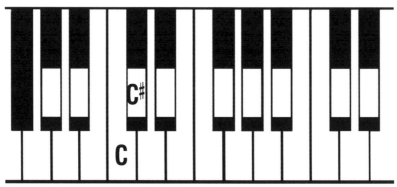

Theory for Everyone • Violin Book 2 Worksheets

9. Key of E

A. Write the four sharps for the key of E on the staff according to "**F**at **C**ats **G**o **D**own **A**lleys...", going left to right. Moving down from the top of the staff, starting from the top space, place each sharp on the first line or space for its note that you come to. Check your answer in *Read It #9*.

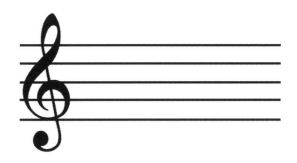

B. Write the names of the notes in a one-octave E major scale from E on the D string to the open E string. Include both 4th fingers and open strings. Only write note-names on the notes that are in the scale; remember the sharps! Play the scale.

C. Write the names of the notes in the E major scale through one octave to the highest E. Include the correct sharps. (Same notes as in B, above.)

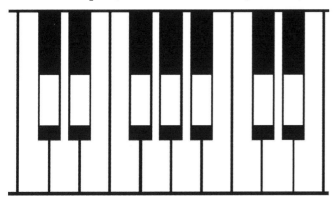

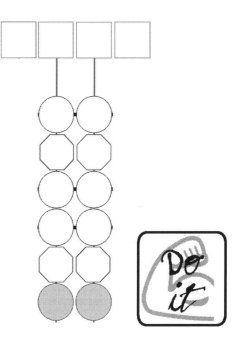

D. 1. Write the key signature for E major as in #9A above.
2. Put a # in front of every F, C, G and D on this staff.
3. Circle all the 3rd finger notes.

Theory for Everyone • Violin Book 2 Worksheets

10. Flats and Enharmonics

A. Review: write sharp names on all black keys <u>above</u> the horizontal line. This range of the piano represents the notes from the open G string to 4th finger on the E string. Find Middle C for reference first if needed. You may also want to write the note-names on all the white keys.

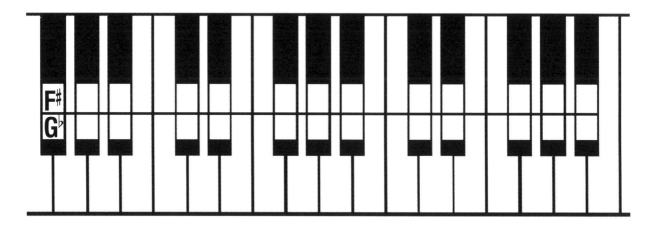

B. Write enharmonic flats' names for all black keys on the keyboard, <u>below</u> the line.

C. Name the flats in these key signatures based on the line or space on the staff where they are located. The order in which to write the names is from left to right.

_____   _____   _____   _____

11. Low 4's

A. On this keyboard, label the black notes <u>below</u> (i.e. to the left of) each open-string note with <u>both</u> their enharmonic <u>sharp</u> and <u>flat</u> names. (G♭ is not included, because there is no note lower than open G on the violin.)

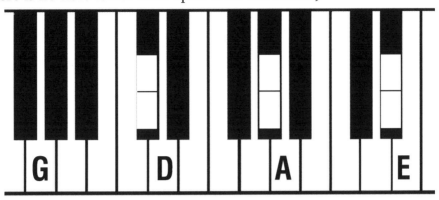

B. Name the 3's, Low 4's and regular 4's on the fingerboard; use enharmonic <u>flat</u> names for the Low 4's.

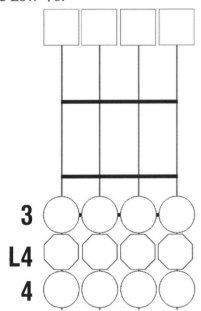

C. Label the note that can be played with <u>either</u> High 3 or Low 4 with <u>both</u> of its enharmonic names (sharp/flat).

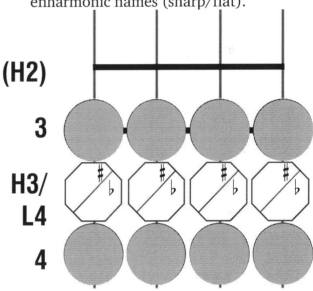

D. In the blanks below the notes, write if you would usually play these notes as a Low 4 (L4) or a High 3 (H3) based on the note and the accidental.

Can you write a rule for when to use a High 3 and when to use a Low 4?

_____

Theory for Everyone • Violin Book 2 Worksheets

12. Low 1's

A. Name the open string, regular 1 and Low 1 notes. For Low 1's, give both the enharmonic <u>flat</u> and <u>sharp</u> names, if there are any.

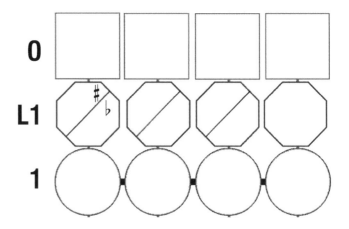

B. Find and label the same notes as in A above on the keyboard. Give the Low 1 notes both of their enharmonic names.

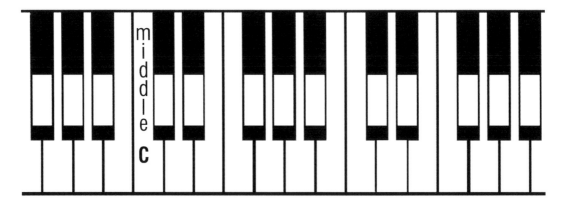

C. Label the notes you would play in the key of C, from open G string to 4th finger on E string. Only label the notes that are in the key — in other words, only the <u>natural</u> notes. Include 4th fingers as well as open strings.

On which string do you play a Low 1?

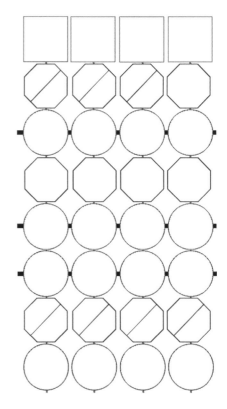

13. Keys of F, B♭, E♭

A. Add the first three flats to the key signature according to B-E-A-(D), writing from left to right. Place each flat on the first line or space for its note that you come to as you move down from the top of the staff. Check your answer in *Read It #13*.

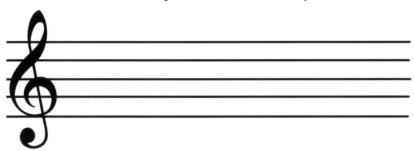

• In the next three exercises, use only the flat names for the (enharmonic) first-finger and fourth-finger notes.
• If you're not sure how to build these major scales, refer to the major tetrachord pattern of whole and half steps in *Read It #1*.

B. Write the names of the notes in a one-octave <u>F major scale</u> *from* F on the D string *to* F on the E string.
How many notes had flats? _

C. Write the names of the notes in a one-octave <u>E♭ major scale</u> *from* E♭ on the D string *to* E♭ on the A string.
How many notes had flats?___

D. Write the names of the notes in a two-octave <u>B♭ major scale</u> *from* B♭ on the G string *to* B♭ on the E string.
How many notes had flats?___

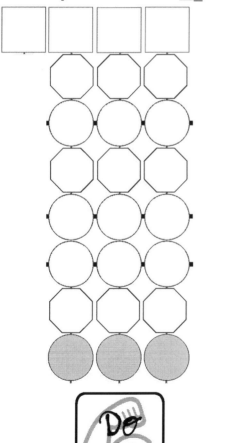
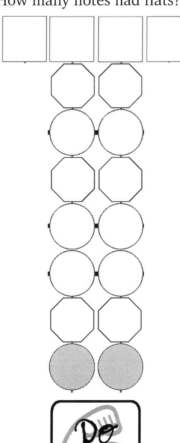
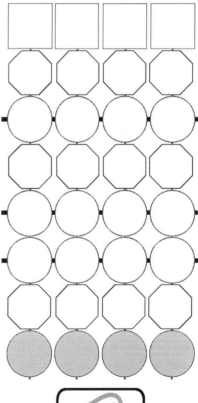

Theory for Everyone • Violin Book 2 Worksheets

14. Minor Scales

Construct these one-octave minor scales starting on the open D string. First write the note-spacing pattern (numbers 1 through 8, using dashes between numbers where there are whole steps) for each type of minor scale, then write note-names on the correct finger positions for the notes in each scale. Only write a note-name on the fingerboard chart if that note belongs in the scale.

A. D natural minor
Spacing pattern:

_____

B. D melodic minor
Spacing pattern:

Up:_____

Down:_____

C. D harmonic minor
Spacing pattern:

_____

15. Important Intervals

Use the keyboard or fingerboard chart to answer these questions. Label the notes first if it will help you answer the questions.

A. What note is a perfect 5th <u>up</u> from A? _____

B. What note is a perfect 5th <u>down</u> from A? _____

C. In first position, how can you play a note that is one octave above the open G, D or A string? _____

D. What note is a <u>major third</u> above D? _____

   What note is a <u>minor third</u> above D? _____

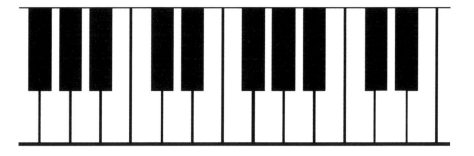

E. TEACHER'S CHOICE: Add your own questions and answers.

_____

_____

_____

_____

_____

_____

16. Sixteenth Notes

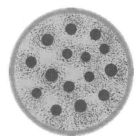

A. Divide a pizza into 16 equal pieces.
How many 16ths in an 8th of the pizza? _____
In a quarter? _____ In a half?_____

B. Write the counting below these rhythm patterns combining quarter, eighth, dotted quarter and sixteenth notes. Insert the bar lines.

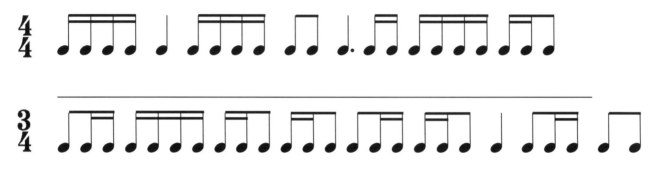

17. Dotted Eighth-Sixteenth Notes

A. Write the counting for each set of 4 beats. Insert the bar lines.

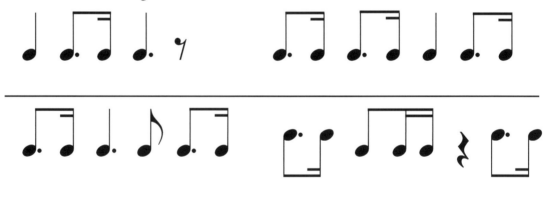

B. Write the counting and insert the bar lines. Can you identify this familiar tune by its rhythm?

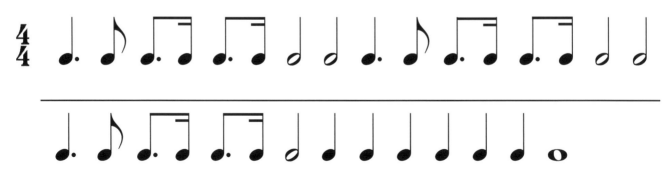

Theory for Everyone • Violin Book 2 Worksheets

18. Triplets

Write the counting of these measures with triplets, and insert the bar lines.

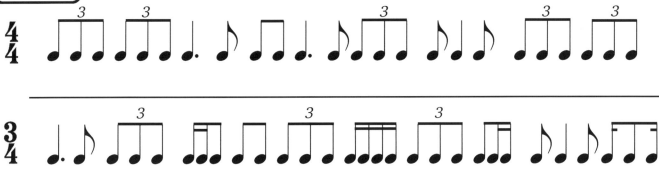

19. Note-Name Review

A. Fill in this fingerboard chart completely, including the enharmonic names of the note-positions with diagonal lines through them.

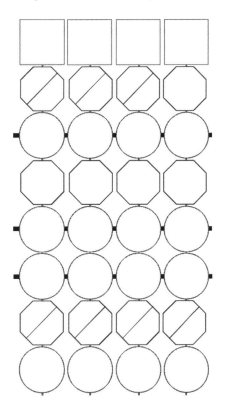

Congratulations! You have learned all the possible notes that can be played in first position!

B. Play a chromatic scale with the notes you labeled in part A.

Theory for Everyone • Violin Book 2 Worksheets

20A. The Circle of Fifths: Order of Sharps

Fill in the blanks with the names of the major keys in the correct positions, including sharps and flats.

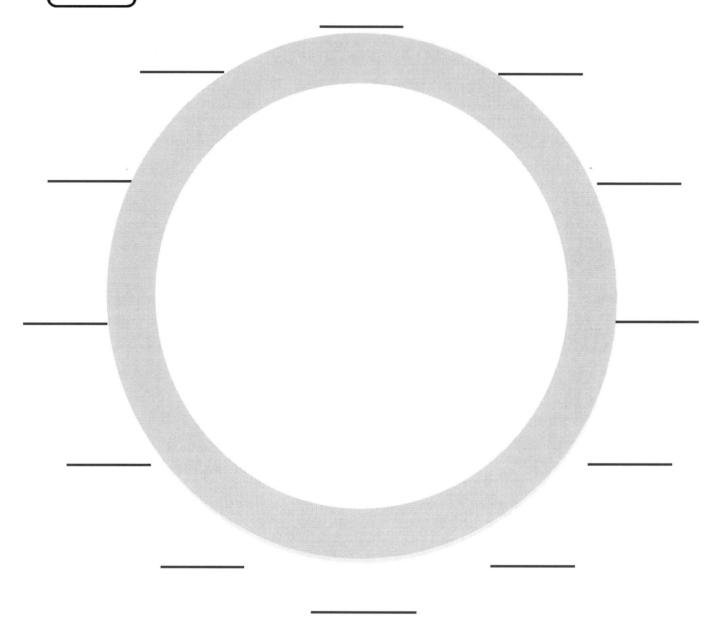

The order of Sharps:

___ ___ ___ ___ ___ ___ ___

20B. The Circle of Fifths: Order of Sharps AND Flats

Fill in the blanks with the names of the major keys in the correct positions. Fill in the boxes with the number of sharps or flats in each key (i.e. "3♭" for 3 flats).

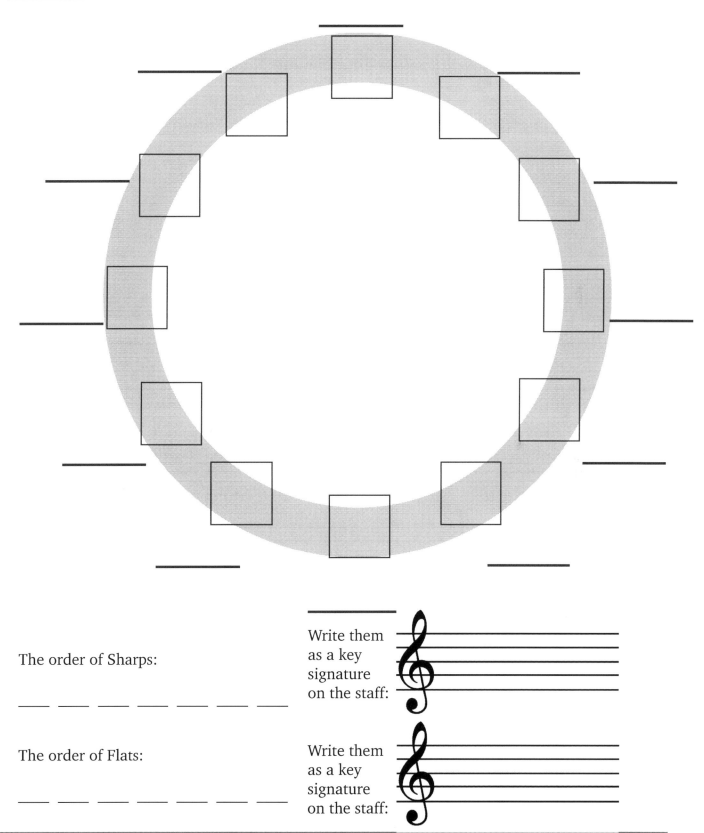

The order of Sharps:

__ __ __ __ __ __ __

Write them as a key signature on the staff:

The order of Flats:

__ __ __ __ __ __ __

Write them as a key signature on the staff:

Theory for Everyone • Violin Book 2 Worksheets

21. The Circle of Fifths: Relative Minors

Fill in the upper blanks with the names of the major keys in the correct positions and as CAPITAL LETTERS. Fill in the boxes with the number of sharps or flats in each key (i.e. "3♭" for 3 flats). Fill in the lower blanks with the relative minor of each major key, in lower-case letters.

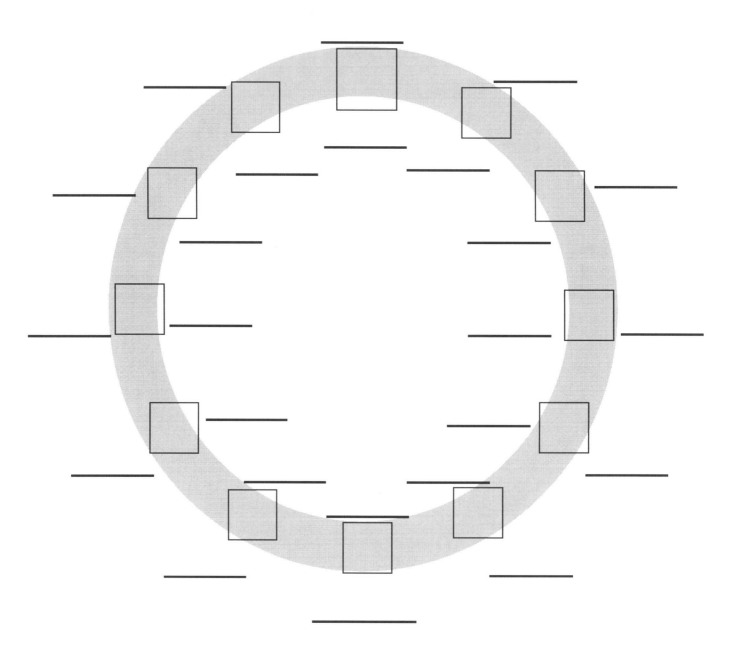

22. The Circle of Fifths: Related Chords

Fill in the upper blanks with the names of the major keys, then answer these questions:

A. What are the I-IV-V chords for the key of C? _____

B. What are the I-IV-V chords for the key of D? _____

C. What are the I-IV-V chords for the key of B♭? _____

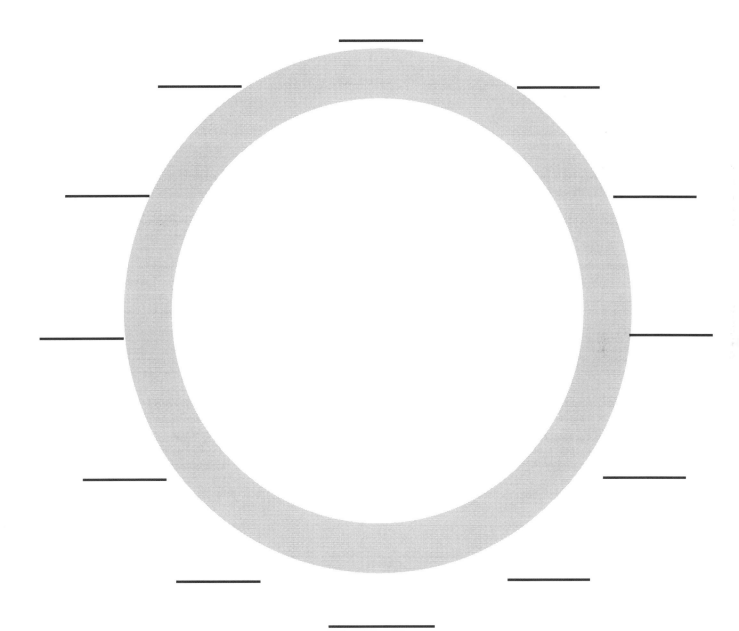

Glossary of Terms Used in Book 2
that were not introduced in Book 1

Beam A horizontal bar that joins together several sequential eighth or sixteenth notes, or any notes shorter than quarter notes

Degree (of scale) The distance in number of notes that a given note is from the root or bottom of a scale

Enharmonic Tones that have the same pitch but are named or written differently depending on the key in which they occur

Fifth An interval of five notes, counting the first note as "1", with all the notes in the same key

Flat Part of the name for a note which is a half-step lower than a natural note; or, to be lower in pitch than a target note

Interval The distance between two notes, expressed as a number or degree (2nd, 3rd, 4th etc.)

Key signature The written indication at a beginning of a piece of music of the sharps or flats to be played in the music; it also tells the musician which major or minor scale is the source of the notes in the music

Major A type of scale or key that uses notes which follow a specific pattern of whole- and half-steps from the root note of the scale: 1-2-34-5-6-78 (two major tetrachords)

Minor A type of scale or key that uses notes which follow a specific pattern of whole- and half-steps from the root note of the scale, different from the major (above). There are three flavors, each with its own note-spacing pattern: **natural**, **melodic** and **harmonic**

Mode A general name for a specific patterned arrangement of notes to form an 8-note scale. **Major** and **minor** are the modes most commonly used in western music.

Octave An interval of eight notes, counting the first note as "1", with the notes in the same key

Syncopation An uneven musical rhythm marked by short-long-short rhythm patterns

Tetrachord A group of four notes which is a building block for major and minor scales

Third, major The name for the interval of two notes which are 4 half-steps (two whole steps) apart

Third, minor The name for the interval of two notes which are 3 half-steps (1½ whole steps) apart

Triplet A group of three notes that divides a quarter note into three equal rhythmic parts. (*In this book, only eighth-note-triplets are introduced.*)

Theory for Everyone Book 2 Answer Key

#1:

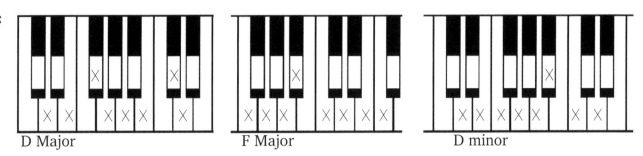

D Major   F Major   D minor

#2: **A.** See *Read It #2* for fingerboard diagram

B.

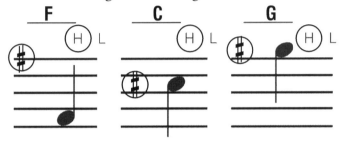

C. HHHL   HHLL   HHHH   HLLL   LLLL

#3: **A., B.** See *Read It #3.*

C.

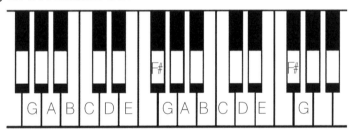

#4: **A.** Ⓐ B C#̸ D Ⓔ F# G# A

B. A C# E A C# E A C# A E C# A

C.

#5: **A.**

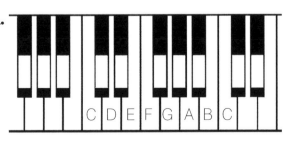

B. See *Read It #5.*

#6: "The Entertainer" (Scott Joplin): 12-3-4-& | 1-&2-&-3&-4-& | 123-&-4-& |
1&-2-&3-&4 | 123-4 |

#7: **A.** 2, 1, 4, 3, 6; 1, 2, 4, 6, 3   **B.** 1234-5-6 | 12-3-4-5-6 | 12-3-45-6 | 12-3-4-5-6 |
12-3-4-5-6 | 123-456 | 123-456 | 1-2-3-45-6 | 123456
"When Johnny Comes Marching Home" (second half of verse)

#8: **A.** See *Read It* #8.   **B.** 1) C, G, D   2&3) 2nd space down, top space, 2nd line down
C. H L L L; H H H L; H H L L   **D.** G#, A#, C#, D#, F#, G#, A# etc.

#9: **A and B.** See *Read It* #9.   **C.**

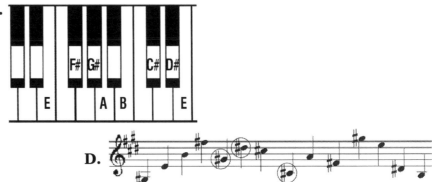

D.

#10: A, B. (continue the pattern)

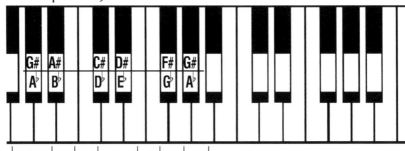

C. B♭ | B♭, E♭ | B♭, E♭, A♭ | B♭, E♭, A♭, D♭

#11: **A.** C#/D♭, G#/A♭, D#/E♭
B. G string: C, D♭, D | D string: G, A♭, A | A string: D, E♭, E | E string: A, B♭, B
C. Same answers as **A**; add A#/B♭ on E string
D. Sharps = High 3's Flats = Low 4's. Rule: Use 3rd finger when the note without the accidental
would be played with a 3, and 4th finger when the note without the accidental would be played with 4.

#12: **A.**

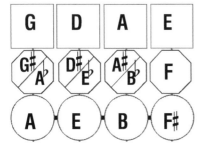

B.

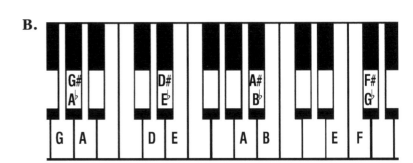

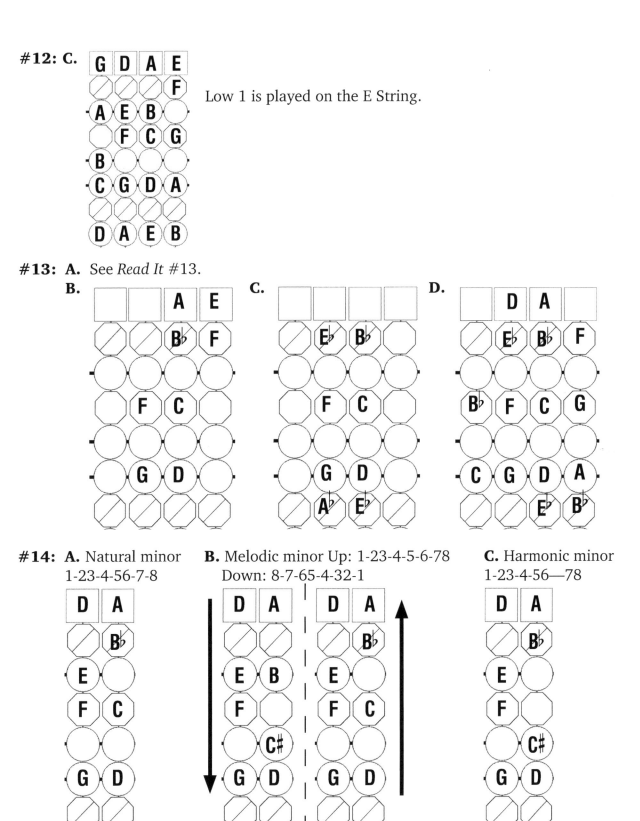

#12: C. Low 1 is played on the E String.

#13: A. See *Read It* #13.

#14: A. Natural minor 1-23-4-56-7-8 **B.** Melodic minor Up: 1-23-4-5-6-78 Down: 8-7-65-4-32-1 **C.** Harmonic minor 1-23-4-56—78

#15: A. E **B.** D **C.** Play the 3rd finger on the next higher string. **D.** F#, F

#16: A. 2, 4, 8 **B.**

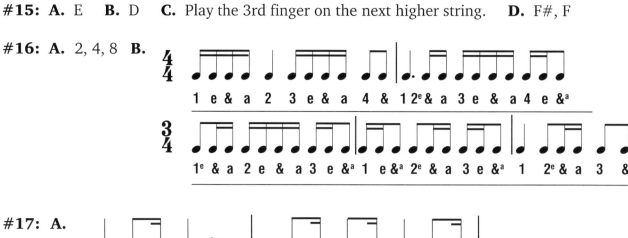

#17: A.

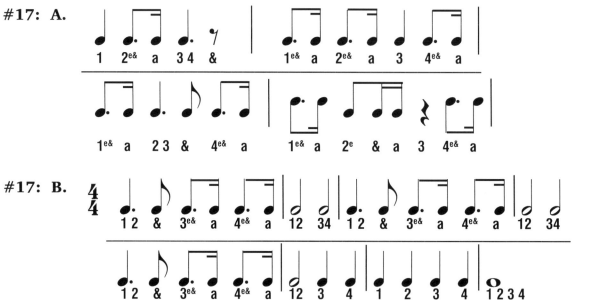

#17: B.

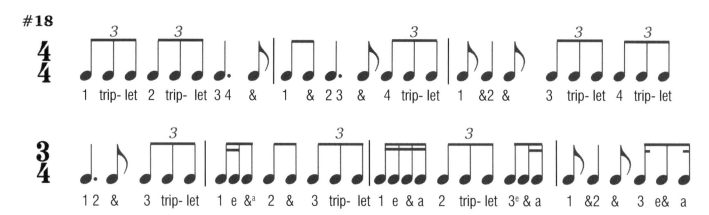

This is the rhythm for "Battle Hymn of the Republic" -- chorus "Glory, glory hallelujah"

#18

#19-22: All answers can be found in the associated *Read Its*.

Made in the USA
Columbia, SC
21 August 2022